Introduction to Mystery Shopping

AL HAZLERIG

INTRODUCTION TO MYSTERY SHOPPING

THE PERFECT HOME-BASED BUSINESS

2007

Introduction to Mystery Shopping

TABLE OF CONTENTS

Chapter I	What is Mystery Shopping?	1
Chapter II	Getting Started	3
Chapter III	How to Select Jobs	7
Chapter IV	Doing the Shop	9
Chapter V	Getting Paid	13
Chapter VI	Phishing	15
Chapter VII	Forums	17
Chapter VIII	Merchandising	19
Chapter IX	Frequently Asked Questions	21
Chapter X	Important Websites	25

Dear Potential Mystery Shopper,

Thank you for buying or at least looking at my book. Mystery shopping is a growing field that is what I consider to be the perfect "work from home" opportunity. As you will find if you read my book, mystery shopping requires very little financial investment. Your success as a mystery shopper will be determined by your own efforts.

My goal in writing this book was for you to read the book and be able to start your mystery shopping business immediately. In writing the book, I have made some assumptions. You need to have a computer and Internet access to be a successful mystery shopper. Hopefully, you can begin mystery shopping and making money in just a few days.

If you find this book useful, please go to the Amazon website and write a review about my book. If you have any problems you can email me at ahazlerig@yahoo.com and I will assist you in any way I can.

Thanks and Good luck

Al Hazlerig

CHAPTER I
What is Mystery Shopping?

A mystery shopper is a customer service auditor who, posing as a customer, goes into an establishment and evaluates the service and/or products of the establishment for a fee. There are more than 800 mystery shopping companies in the United States with an estimated income of over $600 million annually. The top markets using mystery shoppers are restaurants, retail, banking/financial institutions and hotels. These businesses use mystery shoppers to evaluate employee knowledge, review their policies and procedures, measure organization performance and to see how their customers perceive their businesses.

Most people who ask me about the mystery shopping class think that when they complete the material, they will then be qualified to seek employment with a local mystery shopping company as an employee of that company. That's not exactly how it works. As a mystery shopper, you are considered an independent contractor. You will shop for several different companies. Sometimes, you will do several shops for the same company for a long period of time. You could also do a shop for a company on a one time basis. You should receive thorough training and a questionnaire before you enter the location for a shop. You will never go into a mystery shop without knowing exactly what you are to do or what you are to evaluate. And the most important thing, the Golden Rule of mystery shopping, is to never reveal yourself as a mystery shopper!

Mystery shopping can be done on a part time or full time basis. Most shoppers use mystery shopping as a supplement to their regular job. Mystery shopping is perfect for retired people who want to continue working or stay at home moms who need extra cash, but also need to set their own work schedule.

CHAPTER II
Getting Started

In order to be a successful at mystery shopping, you must first have three things: a computer, Internet access, and an email account. The email account should be one that you specifically use for mystery shopping and not your personal account. That way, you will not clog up either one with unrelated emails. It would be very useful for you to have a fax and copy machine. There will be times when you will need them.

Almost all mystery shopping companies have websites on the internet. All you have to do is find their websites and apply to these companies as a mystery shopper. Once you are accepted by the company, then you can enter the website, take the training courses available for specific jobs, then select available jobs in your area. After selecting the job, you will do the shop and fill out a report. Then return to the company website, submit the report and the best part, wait for your pay.

I know this all sounds "as clear as mud." So, let's take each part a little slower.

How do you find these mystery shopping companies on the Internet?

Wait a minute. Before I get to that, let me make a suggestion. Never pay to be a mystery shopper. There are companies out there who offer to find the jobs for you at a hefty price. Something like $20 a month. I personally do not believe you need to pay someone a monthly fee for something that is free. That's just my opinion.

Now, back to the mystery shopping companies. There is a website on the Internet that is very helpful for mystery shoppers. The website is www.volition.com. This website has many areas, but we are only concerned with the mystery shopping section. In this section, you will find the websites for most mystery shopping companies listed in alphabetical order. There is also a description of the company, the area of the country that they shop and the types of establishments the company shops. The site will help you narrow your search for companies. As an example, if you live in Memphis, you do not need to apply to a mystery shopping company that only shops on the West Coast.

You must apply to a mystery shopping company to become a shopper. This is simply a matter of giving them a little information about yourself and your interest and experience. You do not have to have mystery shopping experience. Just shopping experience. You should be able to write a report clearly and concisely, with correct spelling. Pretty much anyone can qualify to be a mystery shopper. It is your advancement that will be determined by your shopping ability. The better your shops and reports are, the more shops you will get. And also, the better paying shops will come your way.

Before you go to the mystery shopping websites, I suggest you become certified by the Mystery Shopping Providers Association. The MSPA. You can find the MSPA at www.mysteryshop.org. At this website, you can take a short course on mystery shopping. You then take a test of about 10 to 12 questions and if you pass, you will receive a "Silver

Certification." That is, after you pay a fee of $15. I think this is money well spent. When you apply to mystery shopping companies, one of the first things they will ask for is your Certifications from MSPA. There is also a Gold Certificate, but it is quite expensive. I'm not sure the Gold is worth the money. Maybe, but not for me. There are other certification programs by another organization, the National Center for Professional Mystery Shoppers and Merchandisers. They are more expensive and I have never been asked for those certifications.

Also, when you apply to mystery shopping companies, you will be asked for your Social Security number. This is necessary because you are an independent contractor. You will be issued a 1099 by the mystery shopping company if you earn more than $600 per year. A necessary evil. I have never had any problems with any mystery companies that I have applied to as far as security issues. I feel confident you will not either. I have made a list of mystery companies that I have worked for in the past. These are companies that offer good jobs, require easy reports, and pay promptly. The list is at the end of the book.

An important part of being a busy mystery shopper is applying to mystery shopping companies on a daily basis. Working for several companies will give you a larger number of jobs to choose from. This is especially important for a new shopper. I have shopped for many years and I still apply to different companies.

When applying to mystery shopping companies, there are a few questions that are asked by most companies, so get your answers ready.

1.) Why do you want to become a mystery shopper?
2.) How would you describe a recent positive shopping experience?

3.) How would you describe a recent negative shopping experience?

4.) What area codes or zip codes are you available to shop?

If you have the answers ready for these questions, this will save you a lot of time.

CHAPTER III
How to Select Jobs

Once you have applied to a company, you wait to be approved as a shopper. For some companies, this could be a matter of a few days and for other companies, we are talking about weeks. Here are some examples of how different companies operate.

Company A notifies you that you have been selected as a shopper. You will be a given a username and a password. You then go to the Company A website and look for the jobs available in your area. You will review the specifics for the jobs such as location, timeframe, any special requirements and pay rate. You can then select a job and the job will immediately be placed in your "to do" list.

For Company B, everything is the same until you select the job that you want. As a shopper for Company B, you select from the available jobs, then you wait for Company B to inform you that you have been selected as the shopper who will do the job. You will be notified by email and the job will be added to your "to do" list.

As a shopper for Company C, everything is done differently. Company C requires you to complete a "project review" for the establishments that they shop. Project reviews are summaries of what is expected of you as a mystery shopper doing an audit or shop for the company. They can be very thorough and require more study time. Some also require you to complete and pass a "project exam" before you can select a shop. You will only be required to do one project review and exam for a particular shop. As an example, if you pass the exam to do a Burger World shop, you can then do several shops for Burger World without taking another exam. This sounds like more work for you. But there are advantages. You will learn a lot about mystery shopping. When you complete your reviews and exams for these companies, you can select shops and those shops are immediately added to your "to do" list.

There are, of course, exceptions to these methods. But basically, that is how it's done. It all may sound a little complicated now, but the more you do, the easier it becomes.

CHAPTER IV
Doing the Shop

Now we have jobs on our "Jobs To Do" list. How do we actually do a mystery shop? I'm going to tell you about two of my favorite shops. The first is a movie theater shop. I go to the mystery company's website. Then, to my "to do" list. I click on the movie shop. I read about how the mystery shopping company, let's say Company A, wants the shop done. There will be information about the location of the shop, the time frame for the shop, and the questions that I am to answer. These questions are listed on a form called an "audit form." Research is very important in mystery shopping. I study the questions thoroughly. What names and descriptions do I need to know? What areas of the theater do I need to inspect? One advantage in doing a movie theater shop is the fact that you can carry a notebook and pen with you into the theater and record your answers without being noticed. This is not always the case. On some shops, you will have to rely on your memory until the shop is over and you are back in your car. In these instances, you need to record the information as soon as possible. These are some of the questions on the audit form.

1.) What is the name of the ticket cashier?
2.) Was the cashier polite?
3.) Were you given the correct change?
4.) Were you given a receipt?

5.) How many people were working in the concession area?

6.) How long did you wait in the concession line?

7.) Was the food prepared correctly?

8.) Was the restroom clean and well stocked?

9.) Was there signage in the lobby for coming movies?

10.) Was the lobby clean and free of debris?

Then we chose a movie and enter the theater. The first thing we need to do is count the number of patrons already seated. It is best to get there early to make this count easier. And, of course, do not let anyone know what you are doing. <u>The first and most important rule of mystery shopping is to remain anonymous.</u>

My wife works with me on movie shops. She watches one entrance while I watch the other. We add people to the count as they come in, careful to subtract if they leave.

Now, as we have learned before we do the shop, we must list the four commercials that are shown before the movie and the four previews that are shown. With the help of a pen light, I list these in my notebook. You are not asked to critique the movie that you see, only the name of the movie.

That is a basic movie shop. It is very easy and always enjoyable. You will then go back to your computer at home and file your audit report. This will need to be done no later than 24 hours after the shop. Just go to the mystery shopping company website and click on the job. Then click on "file your audit report." All you have to do is answer the questions and submit the report. In 30 to 60 days, you will be paid a fee which consists of reimbursements for your tickets, your concession purchase and a fee for doing the shop. You may be asked to send in receipts for the purchases, so hold on to those for a few weeks.

The next shop I want to tell you about is a grocery store shop. I like these because I can actually carry my questions to be answered with me. I just write the questions on a folded piece of paper and carry the paper and pen with me as if the paper is my shopping list. This makes the shop much easier.

These are some of the questions you will be asked on a grocery shop.

1.) How many loose carts are in the parking area?

2.) How many checkers are working?

3.) How many self-service lanes are open?

You'll also be asked to interact with employees within each department of the store, such as the meat, pharmacy, dairy, etc. You will be given a set of questions that you can ask.

On the audit form, you will be asked how the employees answered their questions. There is nothing difficult at all about this. You are usually given multiple choice answers to best describe the employee's reactions.

On the grocery shops, you are paid a fee plus a reimbursement of about $10 on your grocery bill. It is an easy shop and helps to pay the grocery bill.

There are a wide variety of shops, too many to mention here. But all are done basically the same way. You are provided with the questions before the shop. All you have to do is provide the answers and submit your audit report to the mystery shopping company. Then you wait to be paid.

Most common areas of questions on a mystery shopping audit:

- Cleanliness of establisment
- Greetings to customers

- Appearance of salespersons
- Effectiveness of presentations by salesperson
- Promptness of service
- Promotions or displays
- Manager or supervisors ability to handle customer problems
- Handling of returns
- Availability of products

CHAPTER V
Getting Paid

Okay, we have done the shop. Now we need to get paid. Mystery shopping companies use different methods for paying their shoppers. Some pay by check. Some use PayPal. Others use automatic bank draft to your checking account. Most companies pay about 30 to 60 days after you do the shop. That seems like a long time, but after you start doing several jobs, your payments will become more consistent. Your bookkeeping system must be precise. I use a three-step method.

1.) Jobs to do
2.) Jobs completed
3.) Jobs with Payment received

If you do not receive payment after 60 days, email the company for an explanation. Maybe they are waiting on a receipt for your purchase associated with the job. Or they could need clarification on timings of a job. Just let them know you have not been paid and I am sure they will report with an explanation. If you encounter a company that is persistently late with your payments, I would simply drop them from my job searches. There are plenty of mystery shopping companies that pay on time.

I mentioned PayPal earlier. PayPal is an e-commerce business that is owned by eBay. People who buy and sell on eBay use PayPal to pay for their purchases or receive payment from their buyers. Mystery shopping companies will deposit your payments in your personal PayPal account. Then you can withdraw your money in several different ways. For more information on PayPay, go to their website, www.paypal.com. There you can find all the information you need and also register with PayPal. As a mystery shopper and an eBayer, I have done a lot of business thru PayPal. And I have never had any problems.

There are basically three different pay structures used by mystery shopping companies:

1.)   Reimbursement for expenses
2.)   Reimbursement of expenses plus a fee
3.)   Flat fee

The reimbursements always have a limit. On a fast food shop, you will be given a choice of meals to purchase and you will be reimbursed for those choices, nothing more. The flat fees can range anywhere from $8 and up. Some cruise ships pay flat fees in the $500 to $1,000 range, but these are very scarce and quite complicated.

CHAPTER VI
Phishing

In writing about PayPal and eBay, I must mention a few things about phishing. Phishing is a technique that crooks and scammers use on the internet to steal your money and your identity. Here is an example.

You receive an email from PayPal stating that you need to update your personal information. "Please click on this address to update your information now." You double click on the highlighted area and are taken to a different page. There you are asked about personal info such as your Social Security number or you bank account number. They might even ask for your mother's maiden name. DO NOT DO THIS.

It is a trick. If you click on this web address within the email, you will be taken to a page that is an exact duplicate of the update page used by the company you deal with, such as PayPal or eBay or the mystery shopping company. You cannot tell the difference in the fake webpage and the real webpage. If you update on this fake page, you will be providing the crook with enough information to cause you all kinds of problems. Never do this!

I can assure you that no company such as a mystery shopping company, PayPayl, etc, will ever ask you to update any information within an email. A legitimate company might send you an email and tell you to go to their website and update your information at their website, not within the email. This is true with any company that uses the Internet. If you have any doubts, just contact the company by other means such as phone or mail.

CHAPTER VII
Forums

One of the most useful tools for all mystery shoppers are mystery shopping forums. Forums are made up of mystery shoppers asking or answering questions about mystery shopping. You can find out more information about mystery shopping from the forums than any other source. Here are some examples of the things that are discussed.

- Payment experience with mystery shopping companies
- Ease of audit forms for different companies
- What retail establishments are shopped
- Suggestions on how to get information from employees without revealing you are a shopper
- What is the highest paying job you have ever done?
- How to handle receipts?
- What to do if you have problems on a shop?
- What is the most frustrating part of the mystery shopping jobs?
- What are the different types of accounting systems used by mystery shoppers?
- What are the overall best and worst companies to work for?

These are just a few examples. You can find out anything and everything about mystery shopping on the forums.

Forums:

1.) Volition Forums at www.volition.com
2.) Mystery shoppers freedom forums at www.forumcityusa.com
3.) MSPA forum at www.mysteryshop.org
4.) www.momsnetwork.com
5.) www.mystiqueshopper.com
6.) www.topica.com
7.) Yahoo groups
8.) Delphi forums

CHAPTER VIII
Merchandising

Mystery shopping is a great way to supplement your income without a large financial investment. Some people claim to make as much as $40,000 per year as mystery shoppers. This may be possible, but certainly not easy. First of all, you would have to live in or near a large market to provide enough shops. You would have to be a very good shopper with excellent skills at arranging your shops. In my opinion, mystery shopping is best for the part-timer.

But there is a way that you might become a full timer. And that is using your mystery shopping along with merchandising. What is merchandising? Some examples of merchandising would be changing the American Greeting Cards in the Wal-Mart from Christmas cards to Valentine cards. Merchandisers might straighten up stock in certain sections of the Lowes Hardware Store. They might demonstrate digital cameras at the Best Buy. There is a wide variety of jobs that are done by merchandisers. Like mystery shoppers, you are employed as an independent contractor by a merchandising company. You might be hired to do a single two-hour job, a job that requires 20 hours a week for six weeks, or even full time. Every job is different.

The best way to become a merchandiser is to go to a website called www.narms.com. This is a national organization for merchandisers that includes a job bank and training courses.

At www.narms.com , you can submit a data profile for free. This is just a simple resume. You don't have to have experience to start as a merchandiser. Usually, the company that hires you will train you for the particular job. Merchandising companies check the Narms website for possible merchandisers in the area of the job they have available. They will then send you an email to see if you would be interested in the job. You then contact the company's representative by email or phone to set up an interview for the job. Merchandising jobs usually pay better than mystery shopping jobs, usually at least $12.00 per hour and sometimes more depending on your experience.

The combination of mystery shopping and merchandising can be developed in to a very nice full time income and is a great opportunity to have your on home-based business.

CHAPTER IX
Frequently Asked Questions

1. How much can I earn as a mystery shopper?
    This varies with the different types of shops. The pay can range from $10.00 for a short, fast shop up to hundreds of dollars for a cruise ship audit. To put the pay on an hourly basis, I would say the average would be $15.00 per hour.

2. How much does it cost to start my mystery shopping business?
    Your start up costs would probably be under $50.00 The only money you would need would be for a purchase that would be reimbursed for the shop. That would be reimbursed in your pay for the shop. You might want to consider certification with the Mystery Shopping Providers Association. This costs $15.00.

3. What mystery shopping companies shop certain establishments?
    When applying to mystery shopping companies, you will be required to sign an independent contractor agreement. This agreement spells out all your legal responsibilities as a mystery shopper. One of the responsibilities is that you not divulge to anyone the clients of the mystery shopping companies or any other information about the shops. This is very important.

4. Can I do mystery shops when I go on vacation?

    Sure. All you have to do is go to the mystery shopping company website and chose the location you would like to shop. All the available shops in that area will be shown. There are no restrictions on where you can shop.

5. Can I bring my spouse along on mystery shopping assignments?

    This would be specified in the job description. Some companies require shops be done alone. Other shops need to be done by couples.

6. Do mystery shopping companies withhold income taxes and social security from my paychecks?

    As an independent contractor, you are responsible for income taxes and social security. Most companies provide you a 1099 form at the end of the year.

7. How long do I have to file a report after I complete a shop?

    In most cases, twenty four hours. If this is not possible, simply contact the mystery shopping company and explain your situation. Most every problem can be worked out.

8. How long does it take to receive my payment for a shop that I have completed?

    The time frame from doing the shop until you receive your pay will be from 2 weeks to 60 days. The average being 30 days.

9. What should I do if my payment from a mystery shopping company is not correct?

    Contact the company and report the problem. If I have consistent problems in this area, I simply don't do shops for that company again. You can find a lot of information about this on the job forums.

10. Can I shop for more than one mystery shopping company?

   Not only can you shop for more than one company, it is absolutely necessary to shop for several companies. You need to sign up with new companies every week. This assures you of an adequate supply of jobs and enables you to be more selective in your choice of jobs.

11. Should I pay someone to find mystery shopping jobs?

   I personally don't think you should pay someone to find mystery shopping jobs. There are good websites, such as volition.com, that have lists of mystery shopping jobs.

12. How do mystery shopping companies pay their shoppers?

   Mystery shopping companies pay be different methods. They use PayPal, direct deposit to your checking account or they might mail your check.

13. Does my pay include reimbursement for my expenses, such as a purchase that I am required to make during the shop?

   Yes, your pay will include reimbursement for expenses for purchases that you are required to make during your shop. This amount will be limited to the amount stated in the job description.

14. How do I write a review of this book on Amazon. com?

   Go to amazon.com and find the listing for

"Introduction to Mystery Shopping." Then click on "Write an Online review." I appreciate your opinion.

Thanks again for reading my book. I wish you every success in your mystery shopping business.

CHAPTER X
Important Websites

www.mysteryshop.org (for certification process)
This is the Mystery Shopping Providers Association

www.ncpmscenter.org
This is the National Center for Professional Mystery Shoppers and Merchandisers

www.narms.com (for merchandisers)
Submit a Data Profile

www.volition.com
This website provides an alphabetical listing of most of the mystery shopping companies in the United States

The following are just a few of my favorite mystery shopping companies. There are many more found at www.volition.com.

www.beyondhello.com
www.certifiedreports.com
www.mysteryshops.com
www.iccds.com
www.jancyn.com
www.questforbest.com

www.serviceevaluations.com
www.experienceexchange.com
www.shopnchek.com

Thanks again for reading my book and good luck with your mystery shopping. If you have any questions, you can reach me at ahazlerig50@yahoo.com

Made in the USA
Lexington, KY
18 September 2014